My First Book of Colours

Alexandra Hoffman

My First Book of Colours

Wishing Star Publishing

Published in Canada, for Global Distribution by Wishing Star Publishing

www.wishingstarpublishing.com

ebook ISBN 978-1-998751-17-4
Paperback ISBN 978-1-998751-11-2

Printed in North America.

This book belongs to ...

Red

Orange

Yellow

Green

Blue

Purple

Pink

Brown

Black

White

Grey

Gold

Silver

Colour Mixing

(Secondary Colours)

Yellow + Blue = Green

Blue + Red = Purple

Yellow + Red = Orange

Do you know the colours?

colour in the circles!

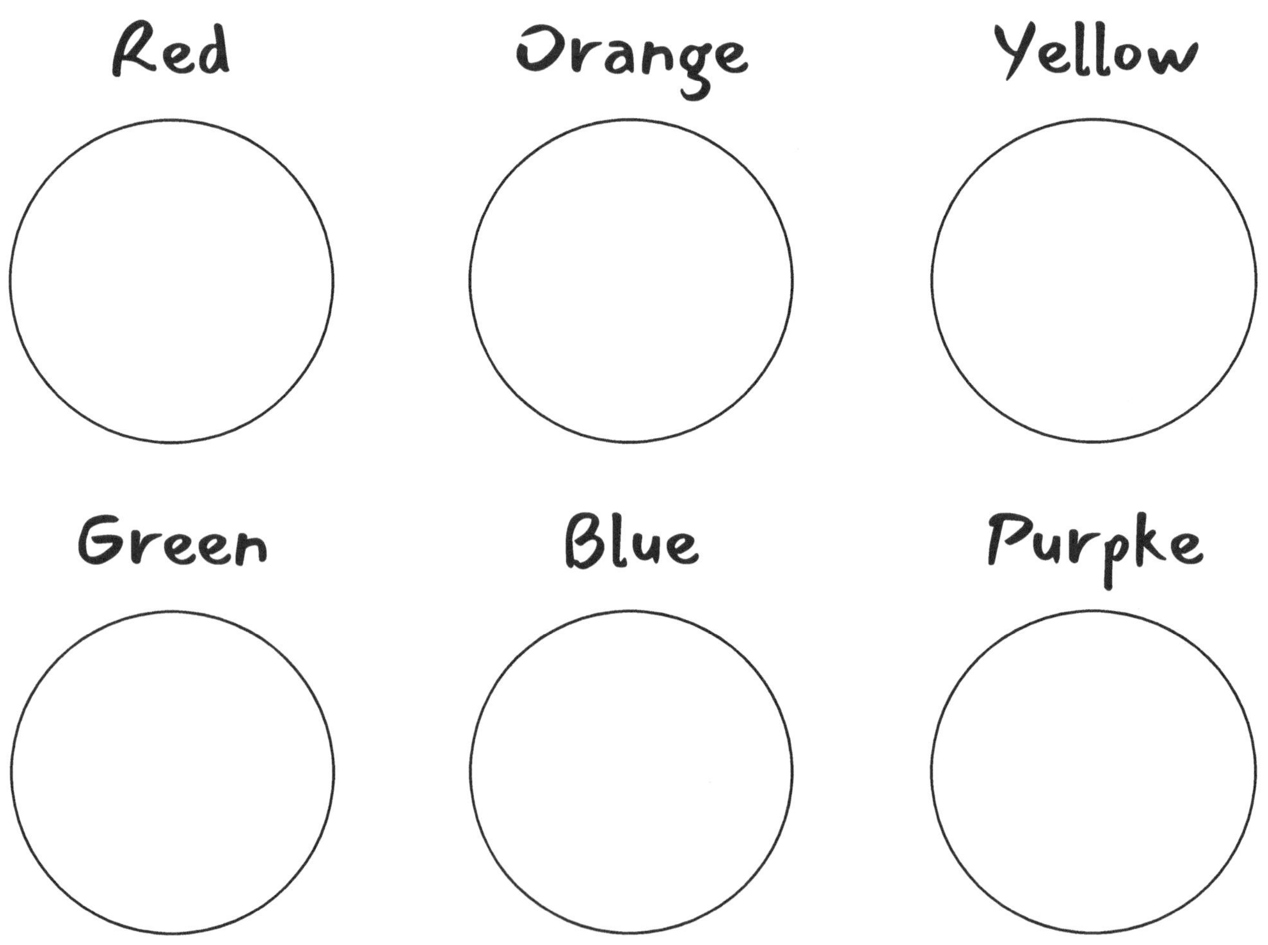

Do you know the colours?

colour in the circles!

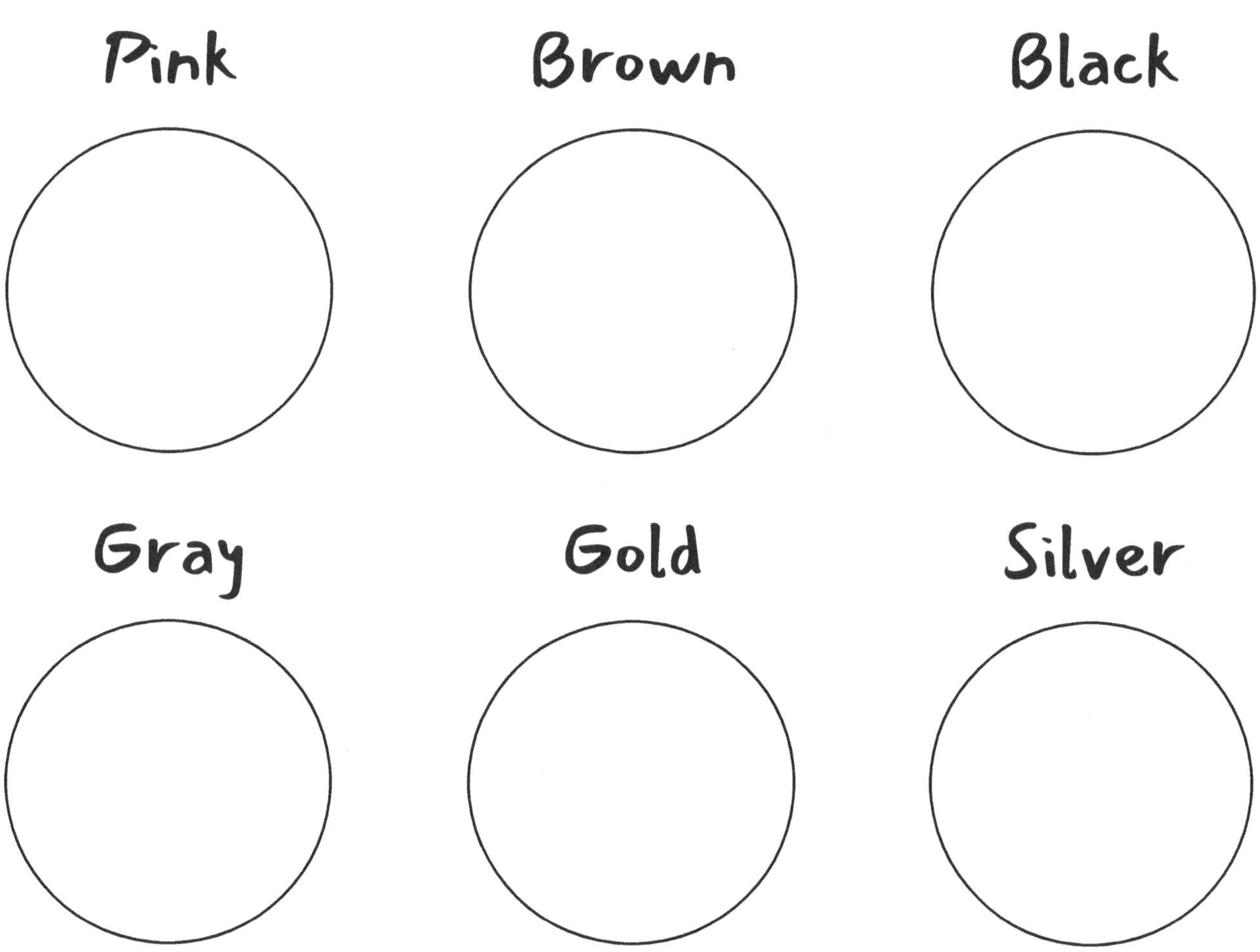

About the Author & Creator of this Book

Alexandra Hoffman is a best-selling author, writer, speaker, mother and founder of Wishing Star Publishing. She is also a teacher with over 12 years of experience in the classroom. The books she writes are dedicated to all the amazing children she has had the honour of teaching over the years and to her family, especially her young son. She lives in Edmonton, Alberta, Canada. Alexandra and all her titles can be found online at www.wishingstarpublishing.com.

If you enjoyed *My First Book of Colours,* it would mean the world if you would take a short minute to leave a heartfelt review on amazon. Reviews are the #1 way others find this book!

Books by Alexandra Hoffman

My First Book of
Colours

Alexandra Hoffman

My First Book of
Shapes

Alexandra Hoffman

My First Book of
Feelings

Alexandra Hoffman

My First Book of
Numbers

Alexandra Hoffman

My First abc Book
Exploring the World Around Me

Alexandra Hoffman

My First ABC Book
Exploring the World Around Me

Alexandra Hoffman

Scan Me!

Alexandra Hoffman

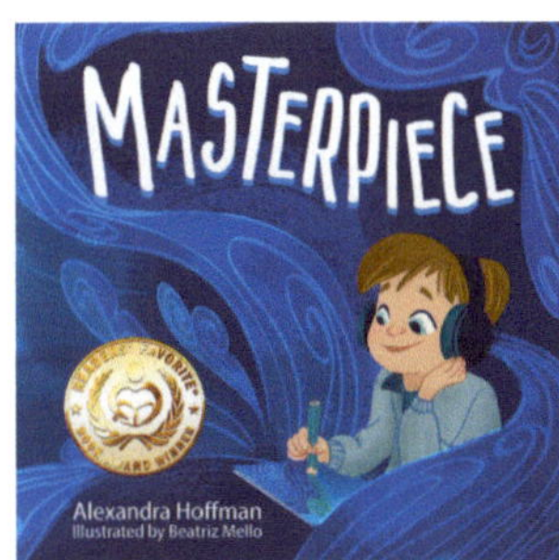

Alexandra Hoffman
Illustrated by Beatriz Mello

by Alexandra Hoffman

A full listing of all titles can be found at www.wishingstarpublishing.com